THE TIDE INSIDE

Written by Katy Towse

Illustrated by Molly Jones

Sometimes in life things are strange,
and hard to understand.
Things don't work out the way you want,
the way you'd always planned.

When someone that you love,
dies and goes away,

it's hard to know just how
to feel, or what to do, or say.

Feelings come and feelings go, without a rhyme or reason.

You might feel different every day, changing like the seasons.

Some days when you wake up,
the tears will flow and flow,
as the river deep inside you
tries to find a place to go.

Other days volcanoes grow,
the lava spilling out.
You can't control your anger,
so you rage and scream and shout.

There could be a tornado,
swirling in your mind.

Asking lots of questions,
the answers hard to find.

But some days there are sunbeams,
shining from your tummy.

Your day is filled with warmth and joy,
making everything feel sunny.

Sometimes there are clear blue skies,
completely normal days.

You go to school, you eat your tea,
you laugh and run and play.

Rainbow days are MAGIC
colours curving up above.
Special days with memories,
of smiles and fun and love.

Just like the deep blue sea,
our feels stretch far and wide.
Up and down, back and forth,
you learn to ride the tide.

Always different, sometimes new,
never for forever,
that's just how our feelings work,
changing like the weather.

So when you're feeling all MIXED up,
when ALL your feelings SHOW
Remember, this is GOOD for you,
it's how your HEART will GROW

TALK it, **SHOUT** it, **DANCE** it.
Just let it all come out.

When feelings stay inside you,
they cause worry, pain and doubt.

FEEL your happy.

TALK your sad.

DANCE your anger.

SING your glad.

ASK your questions

LOUD and **CLEAR**

and **KEEP** your memories

SAFE and **NEAR**

How do YOU feel today?

For Alfie, Evie and Rory.
And for their Grandad,
who made all our days magic.

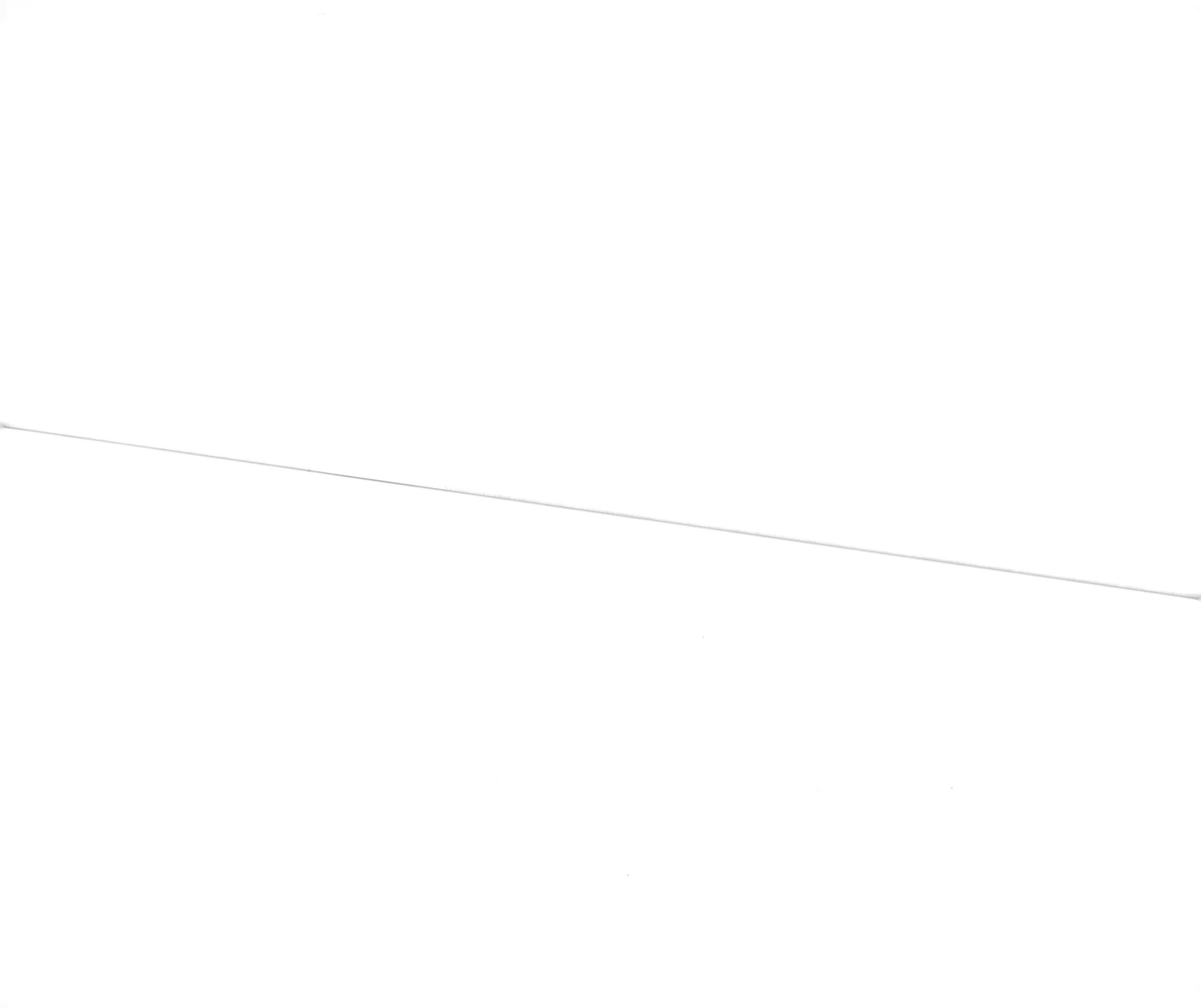

www.ingramcontent.com/pod-product-compliance
Lightning Source LLC
Chambersburg PA
CBHW042107090426

42811CB00018B/1875